Wilbur F. Crafts

A Tour Around the World Among the Temperance Brownies

Wilbur F. Crafts

A Tour Around the World Among the Temperance Brownies

ISBN/EAN: 9783743417489

Manufactured in Europe, USA, Canada, Australia, Japa

Cover: Foto ©Andreas Hilbeck / pixelio.de

Manufactured and distributed by brebook publishing software
(www.brebook.com)

Wilbur F. Crafts

A Tour Around the World Among the Temperance Brownies

A
TOUR AROUND THE WORLD

AMONG THE

TEMPERANCE BROWNIES.

WITH BLACKBOARD ILLUSTRATIONS.

BY

MRS. WILBUR F. CRAFTS,

AUTHOR OF "BLACKBOARD TEMPERANCE LESSONS," NOS. 1, 2, 3, ETC.

NEW YORK:

The National Temperance Society and Publication House,

58 READE STREET.

A Tour Around the World Among the Temperance Brownies.

CHAPTER I.

THE AMERICAN SOUTHLAND, THE WESTERN PRAIRIES, AND CHINA.

WHAT a funny folk the brownies are! And you see they belong to every tribe and nation, but they are "brownies" everywhere, whether they live in China, India, Germany, or any other country. Suppose we make a tour of the world and visit the brownies. This will be a temperance tour, because we are not going to take any wine, beer, or

A Southern Brownie.

any kind of strong drink, no matter if we do find it very cheap or even given away. Some persons who are good temperance folks at home yield to temptation when wine is offered to them free or very cheap in foreign lands. The brownies have a way of finding out things; this is why I want that we should take this tour, and ask them how the temperance cause is getting on. Let us now get into our flying machine. In less than a minute we have come to the South-land, and we will ask this darkey brownie how the colored folks are getting on with the temperance question. "I dunno, massa, but dey mos' all likes to take it; dey's good for temp'rance only part of de time."

If we had not remembered that all the brownie folk are teetotalers we might have thought our black brownie had been taking something himself, he looked so gay and happy. We asked him if it would not be well to have the temperance pledge shown to all of his people. "Yes, massa, but not all of 'em knows how to sign their names, and they forget so soon when 'lection comes." "Are there no black folks for temperance?" "Oh, la! yes, sah, massa, they tries mighty hard." "Help them to try," we said, as we seated ourselves in our flying machine.

An American Indian Brownie.

It does not take long to go from Southland to Prairieland, and that is where the Indians live. Let us call out the chief of the Indian brownies. "White men make good laws; no white man sell Indian 'fire-water,' or give fire-water to Indian. Must pay $300, and go to jail two years. But white man sell Indian fire-water all same. Make bad Indian; Indian get drunk, fight, and kill."

We remembered that we had heard a great deal about the terrible deeds of "drunken Indians." And we remembered too that there have always been good white men in our land who have been trying to have liquor kept from the Indians. The Indians do not make any of it themselves; it is all furnished them by wicked white men, and such poor stuff it is and so full of poisons that a great many Indians have died because of it.

Not all Indians are drunkards.

"How do you think we can help the temperance cause among the Indians?" we asked our brownie. "Let Indian boys and girls learn temperance in schools, and make all white men who come to our country leave their whiskey at home." "We think you are quite right about it, and everywhere in our land we will talk about it when we get back. Good-by."

Now we have crossed the ocean, for as the flying machine goes through the air it does not matter whether it moves over water or land. And here we are in China. None of the Chinese brownies were killed in the war with Japan, neither did they run away. Brownies do not grow old like folks.

This little Chinese brownie was living two thousand years before the Christian era, and he will tell you that even then people in his country were getting drunk. But that now something even worse than drunkenness has come upon them, and that is the use of opium. "You are Americans?" says this little brownie. "Well," he says, "I am glad that in the treaty between the United States and China there is an agreement that no one in the United States will be allowed to send opium to China, and that no Chinaman shall be permitted to bring opium into the United States. We are glad too because opium is a poison that destroys everything that is good in people who take it." Brownie sighed and said: "How we wish that England had made such a treaty with us. It is England that made us buy her opium when we did not want it, and our greatest statesmen would have fought against it if our nation had been as strong as England."

A Chinese Brownie.

NOTE.—Brownie Temperance Sewing Cards. Brownies in outline, to be stitched in bright colors by the children in kindergarten fashion, have been prepared by the author, and may be ordered of the National Temperance Society and Publication House, 58 Reade Street, New York City. 12 cents per set of 12 different Brownies, or 10 sets for $1.00.

CHAPTER II.

INDIA, JAPAN, AND AUSTRALIA.

NOW we proceed on our journey and land in India, and meet a friendly brownie riding on an elephant.

"Please, Mr. Brownie, stop your elephant long enough to tell us how temperance is getting on in India." "You want the latest news, do you? Well, I am not sure whether it will make you angry or make you cry. A company of men were sent over to India from England to investigate whether or not opium was doing the harm that missionaries say it is. They were supposed to be wise men, but we brownies call them 'fools,' for they went home and reported that opium was not doing any harm in India, when in fact it is killing thousands of people every year, and making tens, yes, hundreds of thousands perfectly worthless. They reported also that all of the people in India were willing to have opium sent to India and raised there, when in fact there are Christian people of India who are doing everything they can to prevent the English government from allowing opium to be sent to India. The commission also reported that it was not worth while to try to stop the opium business in India, that it could not be done!" "Do the brownies of India ever take opium?" we asked. "I should think not," he replied indignantly; "it would puzzle anybody to find us to sell us opium, and you may be very sure we would not go where it is and help ourselves."

An East Indian Brownie.

It was a long speech, and the elephant was tossing his trunk and swaying his body as if he wanted to go, so we exchanged *salaams* with our brownie friend, and climbed into our flying machine to take a long journey.

Bless us, this is pleasant, aflying in the air. What is that over yonder? It is surely *Fuji Yama*, the sacred mountain of Japan. What a store they do set by it in Japan! They embroider it, they paint it, they work it in bronze.

Well, we have alighted in Tokiyo, and the Mikado (king)

A Japanese Brownie.

of the Japanese brownies will give us an audience. He has come over two hundred miles in his *jinrikisha* to meet us. "You have a brave people," we say, "and we think Japan may be one of the greatest nations of the world if her people will let strong drink alone. Are there many drunkards among the Japanese?" "Yes. Our people make liquor out of rice," he said, "and it is called *saki*. It makes men mad drunk, and that is worse than 'dead drunk.'" "Rice is much used for food in Japan, is it not?" we asked. "Yes," replied the Mikado of the brownies, "but the people use about one-seventh of all the rice they raise for making *saki*." "Is nothing being done for temperance in Japan?" we asked. "Oh, yes," he replied, "the best people we have in our country are working for temperance, and of course the missionaries do all they can to bring about total abstinence and prohibition." "Thank you, and good-day to your Royal Highness," we said, and pretty soon we were high ourselves, high up in the air, and flying away to Australia. We go on the wings of the wind, you know, and one, two, three, four hundred miles more or less seem like nothing at all. What manner of brownie will meet us this time, we wonder? We had hardly had the thought before we had landed in Sydney. Verily, we thought we were in London town, the buildings were so strong and massive. It seemed all the more like London when we saw the dapper little brownie, who introduced himself as " Algernon Charles Lovelace." We didn't say it, but we did wonder if that one eye-glass of his wouldn't give him rather a one-sided view of things ; but we soon found that he had taken an all-around view of the temperance movement, for he told us that saloons are closed on Sundays in every part of Australia except one, in South Australia, and there the saloons are closed a part of the time on Sunday. "We do not allow liquor to be sold to children under sixteen years of age," said he. " Well, there must be some wide-awake temperance workers in Australia." " Yes, indeed," said he ; "for nearly sixty years they have been working at it ; before that time drunkenness was terrible in Australia ; both the state and the Church were founded on liquor. It is even said that one of the first churches built in Australia was paid for in rum !" " Will you not try to get prohibition ? " we asked. "Of course we brownies would like that," said he, "but our people seem to be more in favor of local option ; that is, to let the people vote whether or not they will have liquor sold in the towns and cities where they live." " Thank you, Mr. Algernon Charles Lovelace, time is flying, and so must we be. Good-day."

An Australian Brownie.

CHAPTER III.

FRANCE, GERMANY, AND HOLLAND.

NOW we have come to France. As you might expect, the French brownies are very polite in all their ways, so we will have to look to our manners. We must prefix every question we have to ask with *S'il vous plaît* (if you please). It would be well for us if we would do this in each and every land.

"If you please, Monsieur Brownie, will you tell us how temperance stands in sunny France? We have been told that French people drink a great deal of wine, but that there is really little drunkenness in your land."

"It is true that our people do drink a good deal of wine. It costs very little; but it is not true that there is no drunkenness in France, although the people do not get drunk on wine. The wine creates a taste for something stronger; absinthe is the liquor that makes the mischief. It is a bitter kind of brandy—tastes worse than the bitterest kind of medicine—but, strange to say, people who drink it learn to like it. It is sold in the cafés (restaurants). Absinthe is the worst enemy France has. It will do more than any foreign foe can to kill off her strong men. Brownies know better than to taste the vile stuff."

A French Brownie.

"Thank you exceedingly, Monsieur Brownie. Good-morning."

We mount our flying machine again, and in the twinkling of an eye we find ourselves in Germany. Truly, we are in good fortune, for here is the drum-major of the brownies. The roll of his drum is so loud he does not hear us speak at first.

"If you please, Herr Brownie, will you tell us how temperance stands in your land? We know that your people drink a great deal of beer, but we have sometimes heard beer called a temperance drink!" "Well," he said, "we brownies know that beer does not help temperance in Germany. You will know this is so when I tell you that in Germany there is a public house (saloon) to every 175 people. We have been told by other brownies it is not so in any other land. Then, women and children drink beer and wine. Some young men in the universities drink as many as thirty mugs of beer in an evening, and large mugs they are, too. On Sundays people go to church in the morning

A German Brownie.

and to the beer-gardens in the afternoon. The streets are full of drunken people." "What a dreadful picture you have given us, Herr Brownie! Do tell us, are there no people in Germany working for temperance?" "Oh, yes, but they do not go about it in the right way. You see they do not work for total abstinence and prohibition, but only for moderation and restriction. We brownies are all teetotalers, and we know that there is no such thing as making people temperate by letting them have fewer saloons." "Surely you are 'exceeding wise,' Herr Brownie. Good-day!"

When next we alighted from our flying machine we were in Holland. You may be sure we felt quite startled when we saw a brownie with a little brown jug. It puzzled us, because we had heard that the brownies in every land are temperance folk. "Pray what have you in your brown jug, Herr Brownie?" "Nothing at all; it is empty, but I am going to buy some water." "Water?" we asked, in surprise; "is there not water, water everywhere in Holland?" "Yes, but there is none to drink; it is sea-water, and so our people have to send barges off to bring it to us, and then we must buy it." "Where do they get it?" we asked. "From rivers that run through the centre of Holland, far away from the seacoast." "Do all of the people in Holland carry water in their little brown jugs?" we asked. "I fear not," he replied. "Is there anybody working for temperance in your country?" we asked. "Oh, yes," he said. "About forty years ago a good clergyman translated from the English some good temperance books, and these, together with the Bible, have been put into the cell of every prisoner in Holland." "What a wise thing to do," we said, "because in America we are told that nine-tenths of all the crime committed is through drink.

A Holland Brownie.

Are there any temperance societies in your country?" we asked. "Yes, there are," he said. "We call such societies *Veresniging tot Afschaffing van sterken Drank.*" We tried to speak it after him, and it almost split our throats. We would gladly have had a drink of water from his little brown jug, if it had been full.

CHAPTER IV.

ENGLAND; IRELAND, AND SCOTLAND.

WHAT a wonder it is that men have been so long a time inventing the flying machine.   It makes the railroad train seem like an old slow coach.   We were in Holland only an hour ago, and here we are in London town, where the Prince of the English brownies lives.   The first sight we got of him, we snapped our kodak at him, and had his picture, three feathers, crown, ermine, and all.

"Is it true that English people are fond of their ale?" we asked.   "Well, they do have a great many ale-houses," he answered, "but there are many people in England, particularly among the great and noble, who would like to do away with the ale-houses and all kinds of public houses."

"Listen while I sing you a bit of a song," he said.   "Canon Wilberforce wrote it:

An English Brownie

   " 'Twinkle, twinkle, bit of blue,
      Witness that I will be true ;
      Symbol of a cause so high
      That angels watch it from the sky.' "

As he sung, he turned back his ermine cape and pointed to his temperance bow of blue ribbon.

He told us that the friends of temperance had grown tired of waiting for Parliament to make temperance laws, and had taken the matter into their own hands, so far as their own property was concerned, so that in their districts in London and Liverpool, and other large cities, there was prohibition—no liquor could be bought.

While we were talking with him a wagon passed by us that had on it the strange device, "Brewers to the Queen." "What can that mean?" we asked in breathless surprise. "It means nothing at all," he said, "only that some brewer wants to sell his beer and ale, and has put a lie on his wagon."

We crossed the Irish Channel and landed in Dublin. The speaker of the brownies with his blackthorn stick was

An Irish Brownie.

on hand at once, for he knew that we were coming. Before we had time to ask him any questions he began to tell us about Father Mathew, who nearly sixty years ago began a great crusade against the drinking houses in Ireland. "Would you believe it," he said, "in four years' time he almost made Ireland a temperance country, and there were hardly any prisoners in our jails." "Then tell us, pray, why Ireland is so cursed with drink to-day?" we asked. "It is because there was no prohibitory law," he answered. "In a few years after Father Mathew's crusade the drink business was going on harder than ever." "Is nothing done for temperance now in your country?" "Oh, yes, there are great temperance leagues hard at work, and there are temperance newspapers. Ireland is not so bad as it would be without these. We hope it will grow more and more to be a temperance land, then people will no longer hear about famine and oppression."

We arrived in the Land o' Cakes for an early breakfast. In every land we had found that the brownies dressed just like other folks, and we were not surprised to find the chief of the brownie clan coming to meet us in his tartan and

Scotch bonnet.   We only wondered that he did not bring his bagpipes along to play Scot's " Wha hae wi' Wallace Bled."

" We have heard a good deal about Old Scotch Whiskey. Is there any of it in Scotland now ? " we asked.   " Plenty, plenty, more than is good for them that drink it," he answered.   " One thing will surprise you very much," said he, " if you will stay over one Sabbath in our country.   You will find that all of the saloons are closed on that day, and they have been closed on Sabbaths for more than thirty years.   Travelers (those who have come more than three miles) can, however, get something to drink by ringing the bell or knocking at the door.   It is supposed that they are so weak and faint that they must have something   to   strengthen   them ! "

A Scotch Brownie.

" Foolish creatures," we said, " not to know that to drink liquor will take away their strength instead of making them strong."

" Are there any temperance societies in your country ? " we asked.   " Yes, there are many, and they are all working together to get Parliament to pass a temperance law that will let each town or district have a prohibitory law. Scotch brownies will not have anything to do with Scotch whiskey."   " They are exceeding wise," we replied.   And with a wave of our hands we mounted our flying machine.

CHAPTER V.

MADAGASCAR AND AFRICA.

WE can travel over water just as well as over land in our flying machine. Suppose we visit next the Island of Mad-

Our Flying Ship.

agascar. Swifter far than the swift ships we sped across the Indian Ocean; as free as the air itself were we. Ploughing their way 'gainst time and tide were they, with billows in front of them, billows at right of them, billows at left of them, billows behind them. The fleecy clouds were the only billows on our path, and we passed by them swifter than eagles.

When next we alighted we were in Tananarivo, the capital of Madagascar, and there came out to meet us a brownie who told us that he was one of a company who made their home in the palace of the good Queen Ranavalona. " We like to be there," said he, " because we never see the queen drinking wine herself nor giving any to her friends. She might easily have her palace full of the merry knights of wine," said he, "for of all the liquor made in Madagascar one-tenth is given to the queen." " What does she do with it if she does not drink it, nor give it to others to drink?" we asked. "She just pours it all on the ground," he replied. " Are all of your people as temperate as your queen?" we asked. " A part are," he replied. " The Hovas have prohibitory law. They do not allow liquor to be made or sold in the part of the island where they live."

A Madagascar Brownie

" What kind of liquor is made in other parts of your island?" " I will tell you what kind of liquor used to be made in Madagascar, and then I will tell you what kind is made now. Before the missionaries came here our people used to make liquor out of the sweet sap of trees, but when our king became a Christian he made a law that all such trees should be cut down, so that no more liquor could be made. After that there was no more drunkenness in our island until England and France made our king allow some Englishmen and Frenchmen to make liquor from the sugar-cane which they were growing in Madagascar. In one short year our streets were filled with drunkards and our prisons with criminals." "Could your king do nothing about it?" we asked. " He did all he could; he bought all that he could, and then destroyed it by having the casks that contained it knocked to pieces." " Tell us the name of that brave king." " King Radama I.," he answered. These strong nations that thus bring evil upon weaker nations will surely have their punishment from the God of Nations.

Now that we are so near to Africa, let us take our way to the Congo Free State, and see what is going on there in the line of temperance.

We had only to telegraph to a brownie through the air— no need of telegraph lines or even telephone wires—that

in a few hours we would be there. When we met the little fellow and received his salutation, we hardly knew whether to address him as "Monsieur" or "Herr" or "Senor" or "Mr." His hat made him look like a Frenchman ; his pipe like a German ; his coat and pants like a Yankee ; his shoes like a Dutchman; his guitar like a Spaniard; his eye-glass like an Englishman. One of our party whispered that he was a "Conglomerate," but another more politely said, "He is international." "Pray, do not take offense, good friend Brownie, but will you explain to us your strange appearance ?"

A Brownie in Africa

"Certainly," he said, with the utmost politeness. "We brownies have only been dressing in this curious fashion for the last year or two. We do so because all of the countries represented in our costume have agreed together to restrict the liquor trade in the Congo Free State, not to allow liquor to be sent or to be sold where it is not already done. And when it is done, laws are made that will tax the business so heavily that many men will cease to import or to make liquor." "That is good," we said ; "with that explanation we think your costume very fine and most becoming. But tell us, please, why not only these nations but others as well are so interested not to have liquor sold in the Congo Free State ?" "Because they all were engaged once in sending liquor here, and they saw that sooner or later it would kill off the nations and ruin their trade ; but aside from this, it has shown to Christian people in these nations that a great wrong was being done to a weaker nation."

How sorry we felt as Americans that our country had ever sent liquor to the Congo Free State. In one year alone we sent 737,650 gallons of wine there! Our faces were red with shame as we remembered this. I wonder if the brownie saw that we were in somewhat of a hurry to get away from his country.

CHAPTER VI.

EGYPT AND SPAIN.

"BEFORE we leave Africa let us take a fly to Egypt." No sooner said than done. We remembered having seen at the Centennial Exhibition in Philadelphia in 1876 a sign like this in the exhibit of Egypt:

> **Greetings from the oldest nation of the earth to the newest.**

Our flying machine was halted at the top of one of the great pyramids, for we wanted to see it, and thought it

An Egyptian Brownie.

would be easier to climb down than to climb both up and down. At the base of the pyramid, waiting for us, was the Egyptian brownie. We pressed the button of our kodak, and here we present him to you. "Muhammed Hassaun." "You are not old like your country," we said. He laughed rather slowly as he replied: "No one can ever guess the age of the brownie folk; we were never young, and we never shall grow old." "Were you here in the beginning of Egypt, longer ago than anybody now living knows anything about?" "Yes," he said. "Surely there were no drunkards then?" "Yes, there were, for Egypt, long centuries before Jesus came into this world, was into the business of brewing, or wine-making. If you will look at her grand monuments, you will find pictures of the winepress, and of intoxicated people. It has been going on ever since, but worse than the wine is the hasheesh, made from hemp, to be smoked. It drives our people crazy. To be crazy is even worse than to be drunken, because one gets over being drunk, but crazy lasts." "Is anything being done for temperance in Egypt?" we asked. "Not very much," replied Muhammed. "Instead, I may say the drink habit is increasing; the American missionaries are about the only persons in Egypt who are doing anything in Egypt for temperance." "Water is very scarce here," we observed. "Yes, our people must buy it in the streets, paying even for a small cup full. Sometimes a rich man will buy a skin of water, and call the people to drink free, so that they will pray for him." We thought of our own dear land, and sang as we seated ourselves in our flying ship,

> " I love thy rocks and rills,
> Thy woods and templed hills."

The shores of Spain beckon to us from across the sea. Afar off we can see the gold and crimson of her banners. In the full tide of moonlight we settled down into the Alhambra. The air was vibrant with the sound of the guitar and the mandolin. As it were, treading on a moonbeam, a brownie friend came forth to meet us, and gave his name as Senor Pablo Yglecias.

You see, word had been passed around among the brownie folk in every part of the world that we were coming, and so they were on the lookout for us. We said, "Senior Yglecias, we do not expect to find much drunkenness in Spain, for we have heard that you have a temperate people, but will you explain to us how this came about?" "I am very much pleased to do so," he replied; "our no-

bles do not have the vice of intemperance, and so a bora-
cho (drunkard) is a vulgar, low-bred fellow; so it would
seem that our people have too much
pride to be drunkards." "Well, that is
the best species of pride we ever heard
of, but surely there is some liquor made
and drank in Spain?" "Yes, something like 500,000,000 gallons of vile
stuff called 'wine.' It is made of grape
must, Berlin alcohol, and some other
chemicals. The sherry wine of Jerez
is famous, but it is made-up stuff too."
"Perhaps you can tell us something of
your neighbor Portugal," we said.
"Haven't you heard of the American
banquets they have in Portugal?" We
had to confess that even though we
were Americans we never had heard of
them. "Well," he said, "American

A Spanish Brownie.

banquets were drinking parties, where the men did not get
drunk enough to make beasts of themselves." "America
then was not very much honored in the custom," we could
but remark. "The people in Portugal are not as drunken
as they used to be, because in the army drunken soldiers
are punished most severely, even with death if it is in the
time of war. Another help to temperance is that the sale
of liquor to boys and girls is not allowed." Oh, yes, we
see they do not mean to grow drunkards in Portugal. We
thought of parts of our own land where they do grow them,
and gave a deep sigh, so deep that Senor Pablo Yglecias
cast an inquiring glance at us. But we felt like keeping
our shame to ourselves, and were glad to tell him that in
some parts of our land there is a law that liquor cannot be
sold within two hundred feet of a school-house.

Our flying ship was straining at its moorings, warn-
ing us that we had better get aboard or we might be left.

CHAPTER VII.

TURKEY AND GREECE.

"SHALL we fly East or West or North or South? Turkey is a most interesting country just now; let us go there." And so we set wing for Turkey, bound for the wonderful old city of Constantinople. We had no desire to see the Sultan, but we had heard that the brownies held court on the roof of the SUBLIME PORTE (the great gate), which opens into the Sultan's palace. We thought it best to alight from our flying machine in an olive grove, a mile or more from the palace. We knew that the sleepy-eyed Turkish soldiers would easily mistake our craft for a huge condor.

But the brownies knew better. They did not venture to come down in a company to meet us, but sent as their representative *Abdul Ibrahim*, who greeted us with a very low

A Turkish Brownie.

salaam. To which we responded in American fashion:

"How do you do? glad to see you," and then we each shook hands with him.

"We understand," said I, "that Turkish people are very fond of cold water, that they prefer it to whiskey; is this true?"

The little fellow laughed all over. "Turks no drink whiskey, but *rakee*, and plenty of it."

"But," said one of our party, "we have heard it said that Mohammedans are forbidden by their Bible (the Koran) to drink liquor."

"They must not drink wine," he said; "but the Koran says nothing about *rakee*."

"Do the brownies drink rakee?" we asked.

"Never, never, never!" they answered in chorus from the roof.

The Turkish guard stirred himself a little, but he evidently thought he had heard the twittering of night-birds.

"I suppose there is no wine made in Turkey then?"

Again Abdul Ibrahim laughed, and pointed his wee finger toward the palace and said:

"The 'Sick Old Man' (as the Sultan is sometimes called) in there is glad to get all the revenue he can from it, and his government even tries to increase its manufacture and sale, so that in one year alone $1,370,600 worth of wine was sold, and the Sultan had a fine revenue from it."

"It cannot be true then," said I, "as I have heard, that a boy in Constantinople is safer from the drink curse than if he lived in one of the great cities of the United States?"

Abdul Ibrahim said "he did not think so, for on every hand were places where not only wine and rakee could be had, but opium as well."

We could not help feeling that the American boy is safer than the Turkish boy, because he is taught in school all about the danger to his body of taking alcoholic drinks.

We were about to ask questions concerning the Armenians, the Christian people of Turkey, but Abdul Ibrahim suddenly disappeared, and not one brownie was to be seen on the roof of the "Sublime Porte." Evidently Abdul Hamid, the Sultan, was awake and aware that he was being told on, so we too beat a hasty retreat, for we did not care to leave our heads in Turkey.

"Greece is only next door," suggested our courier, and almost "as quick as a cat can wink her eye" (she doesn't do it very fast, you know!) we were there, under the shades of the Parthenon, Greece's greatest ancient temple. It is all in ruins now, and we looked in vain for the magnificent statues that used to adorn it. While we were wondering which direction to take, a little Greek gentleman made his appearance, and announced himself as "President of the Brownie Republic in Greece." We looked surprised, and he said :

A Greek Brownie.

"King George is not our ruler; by and by the Greeks will learn how much better it is to have one of their own number for a president than to have a foreigner for a king."

"Are the Greeks any wiser about temperance now than they used to be hundreds of years ago?" we asked, for we had read in history that the ancient Greeks were great wine-drunkards.

"You forget," said President Brownie Themistocles, "that there were laws in ancient Greece against drunkards, and that in Sparta boys were made to look on the silly actions of drunken slaves, so that they would become disgusted with wine drinking."

We could not help replying: "We fear, then, that the people who live in Greece to-day are not as wise as those ancient Greeks."

"You are quite right," said the President; "nothing is being done in Greece now for temperance, and more than three thousand acres of our land are covered with grapes for wine."

"How do the brownies feel about this?" we ask.

"Come," said he, "and I will lead you to a place where you may meet them all, and hear them talk"; and so he led us to Mars Hill, that place of meeting for so many centuries, where men have met together to hear of some new thing.

Never was there such a company on Mars Hill as that day, never a company of people so much in earnest that only the truth should be spoken. The brownies declared themselves quite ready to help in a temperance crusade in Greece.

"But how can we do it?" they asked; "for you know we are so small as not to be counted men and women, nor even children."

It was suggested that they might play the part of the foxes, "the little foxes that spoil the vines" on which the grapes are growing for wine.

"If we only could talk as men and women," said they, "we would stir up the Greeks of to-day to be as noble and as temperate as were the Greeks of the olden time, for so might they again be a great nation."

CHAPTER VIII.

ITALY AND PERSIA.

"LET us set wing for Italy next, for," said one of our number, "we have heard that in wine-growing countries there is little or no drunkenness." And as Italy is next to France the greatest wine-growing country in the world, we might expect to find there a temperate people if that is true! One of our party had spent a winter in Rome, and told us that there wine and milk are the same price, from six to eight cents a quart. We determined to make a landing on the *Campagna*, which is just outside of Rome. We felt sure of meeting the brownies there, for there they could live undisturbed by men. It may not much longer be left to the brownies, for men are learning that by planting eucalyptus trees they can drain the marshes, and so make it a safe place to live in. The eucalyptus trees draw up the water of the marshes with their trunks; indeed, they are as good as pumps. This draining of the *Campagna* has so far been accomplished that we were not at all afraid to make a visit there with the brownies.

An Italian Brownie.

In some countries the brownies are a kingly race, but in Italy they belong to the peasantry, so we were not at all surprised to see a brownie step up to meet us as soon as we had landed, looking quite like an animated rag-bag; and yet his rags were tied on in such a jaunty fashion as to make him quite a model for a painter.   He doffed his hat with a feather in it, and gave us his name as Stefano Sebastiana.

"We have been sailing over the vineyards of Italy, and they seem to us to be covering almost the whole land," we said.

"Yes," he replied ; "Italians make from 600,000,000 to 800,000,000 gallons of wine a year."

"How much of this wine do the brownies drink?" we asked.

"Not one drop," he replied ; "we belong to the B. W. T. S."

"What is that?" we asked.

He pointed his finger at us in a comical fashion, and said : "You are temperance folks, and do not know what the 'B. W. T. S.' is! Why, the 'Brownie World Temperance Society,' of course."

"Is there any other temperance society in Italy?" we asked.

"Yes, there is one," he said, "but you would hardly call it a temperance society, because it does not pledge its members to be teetotalers, only to drink moderately."

"Is there much drunkenness in Italy?" we asked.

"Oh, yes," he said, "and sometimes there are such fights in a drink-shop that the chief of police will shut it up for a whole year."

"It is a pity he couldn't shut up such places forever," we said.   "Is the wine-drinking of the people the reason why one will always see a line of beggars at a railroad station, holding out their hands for the travelers in the cars to toss them something?"

"Yes," answered Stefano, "the Italians would not be so poor if they would let wine-making and wine-drinking alone, and raise grain instead for bread. *Addio*," said Stefano, as he saw that we were preparing to take flight.

"Let us visit next the land of the Wise Men," said one of the party. "What wise men?" "Why, those who followed the star that led them to Bethlehem where Christ was born."

Persia lay to the east across the Mediterranean Sea. If we had taken swan's wings instead of eagle's wings, we might have had a sail on the sea; but eagle's wings are swifter and stronger than swan's wings, and so we were not sorry that we had to cross the sea over it instead of in it.

"What do you know about the drinking of liquor in Persia?" we asked of each other.

One recalled the story of Belshazzar's feast, where he set wine before a thousand of his lords, in the golden and silver cups which Nebuchadnezzar had taken from the temple of Solomon. Another spoke of the great feast which Ahasuerus gave, lasting one hundred and eighty days, at which there was "royal wine in abundance," so that the king and his guests were drunk. Another of our party told us the story of how wine-drinking in Persia began: A very ancient king, Jamsheed by name, tried to keep grapes by putting them into a great jar. The grapes rotted and fermented. The king then had the juice bottled up and marked "poison." There was a lady in his palace who drank some of the poison, because she wanted to kill herself. Instead of killing her, it only made her drunk; while she was drunk she felt so happy that she afterward took it all, little by little; and so in Persia to-day wine is called *zahar-i-khosh*, which means "the delightful poison."

A Persian Brownie.

We decided to alight just outside of the greatest city of Persia, Tabriz. *Hassan u Deen*, for so he gave his name, was not long in finding that we had come to pay the brownies of Persia a visit.

" Do you belong to the B. W. T. S. ? " we asked.

" Certainly; all of the brownies in Persia do," he replied.

" We asked him if he had ever heard the story of the *zahar-i-khosh ?* "

"Oh, yes," he replied; " we were living then, and some of us used to look at that drunken woman, aud think what a foolish and wicked woman she was."

" Do the people in Persia to-day drink that delightful poison ? " we asked (for we could not speak the Persian word).

" Not all of them," he said; " there are tens of thousands of people in Persia who have never tasted any liquor, and who would rather die than take it, because they say it would make them unfit for paradise, and displease Allah (God). The Koran declares that in wine ' is great sin,' and that it is an abomination of Satan's work."

In surprise we asked, " Who, then, does drink liquor in Persia ? "

" Hassan replied, " Mostly the Jews and the soldiers, and some Christians."

" Do not the missionaries try to keep Christians from drinking ? "

" Oh, yes," said Hassan; " they nearly all try to get the people to sign the temperance pledge."

It was time for us to go, so we gave the very best salaams we could to Brownie Hassan and mounted our eagles' wings.

CHAPTER IX.

CEYLON AND NEW HEBRIDES ISLANDS.

BEFORE we journey toward the north again, let us touch where spring breezes

" Blow soft o'er Ceylon's isle."

Somebody in our party suggested that our flying machine might get caught on that line called the Equator, as it passes through the middle of Ceylon. Well, we did not get caught, but landed safely at Batticotta. Surely the Garden of Eden could not have been more beautiful than Ceylon is with its date palms, tree ferns, cocoanut and tamarind trees, and beautiful orchids and tea gardens. To be sure, the deadly cobra, that most dangerous of all serpents, is there. So there was a serpent in the Garden of Eden. With a polite *salaam*, a veritable Sinhalese brownie stood before us. He told us that his name was

A Ceylon Brownie.

Kassappu Thamotharurampilly.
Pronounce it if you can. We asked him to allow us to call him "Ceylon," by the name of his country. He smiled in the gentlest manner and nodded "yes." We asked him if many people in Ceylon were killed by the cobras. " Oh, yes," he replied, "but strong drink is a more deadly foe than the cobra. Our people did not use to know anything about strong drink; their religion, when they were Hindus, Mohammedans, and Buddhists, forbade them the use

of strong drink, but England, which we understood to be a Christian nation, sent strong drink to us, that she might make herself rich through the sale of it. It did not matter to England how our people were degraded and ruined in body, mind, and soul by the liquor and by the opium which she is still sending to us, and forcing us to buy by setting up shops all along our roads and streets to tempt our poor people."

"Surely, it cannot be so bad as that now," we said, "after so much has been said and written about England's wrong-doing in this matter?"

"Yes, and the condition of things is not likely to improve, for England will be deceived by the committee who reported that opium is a good thing for India.

"You are Americans, I believe," continued *Kassappu Thamotharurampilly*. "The lectures of your great temperance orator, John B. Gough, have been translated into our language by the missionaries, and they have greatly helped our people to know what a virtue temperance is, so that Christian Sinhalese are teetotalers."

"How glad we are that the brownies in every land are teetotalers," we said.

"Yes," he replied, "they are little upon the earth, but they are exceeding wise."

"Shall we fly east or west, or north or south?"

"There is no use to go further south, for you'll find only fish and sea monsters, and it is quite safe to say they drink nothing stronger than water," remarked the member of our party who had charge of the geography of our trip.

"I am interested in the New Hebrides Islands; let us go there," said one of the ladies. "They lie to the southeast of us in the South Pacific Ocean," said our geographer. "Are there brownies there?" we asked *Kassappu*. "There are brownies in every land under the sun, and they are all temperance folk," he replied. "Well, you may tell the brownies in the New Hebrides that we are coming," said our captain.   No one knows how one nation of brownies communicate with another, but they never failed to do it anywhere.   Our eagle's wings were soon set for the New Hebrides.   Those brave, strong eagle's wings, in every clime, in any land, they seemed to be in their element, fitting emblem of the fact that out of every tribe and nation there are those who come to make their home in America, "the land of the free and the home of the brave."

On, on we flew until at length there came to view, spread out like a great map below us, a group of islands, twenty or more, some of them as much as sixty or seventy miles long, and others much smaller.   On one of them there was a great volcano belching out fire, but for the most part the islands look green and fertile.   We landed on Espiritu Santo, the largest of the islands.   What a tribe of brownies

A New Heb-ides Brownie.

were there to greet us, for you must know that folks of our complexion were a great curiosity in those parts.   One of their number stepped forward to greet us.   "Erramongo" he gave as his name.   We snapped our kodak, and here is the picture we had of him.

"You are so far away from the nations that make and sell rum," said we, "that we expect to hear the islanders are a very temperate people."

"Ah, not so," said he in a sad tone.   "They make *kava* and drink it, at least the men do.   The women are not allowed to drink it because they have to do all of the work."

We had never heard of *kava*, and we asked how it was made.

" From a kind of pepper plant. The boys and girls are made to chew it, and as they chew it they spit it into pans. Then men and women pour water over it and strain it, and set it away to ferment. When it is fermented the men drink it, and then they lie down and sleep as if they were dead. You should see them when they are drinking it," said he. " They spit out the settlings and say ' *Kumesan* '— ' O Devil, here is your share.' "

" Do all of the men in the New Hebrides drink this stuff ? " we asked.

" No," replied Erramongo, " not after they become Christians."

" Has there never been a kava taker among the brownies ? "

" Not one," said he, " for then we should be more filthy than the little hogs that run about our island. Perhaps you do not know about our hogs. We have been told that they are about the size of your rabbits."

" Please let your brothers in the Sandwich Islands know that we are coming to visit them," we said, as we got into our ship and prepared for another flight.

CHAPTER X.

SANDWICH ISLANDS, GREENLAND, AND ICELAND.

" WE can fly east or west to reach the Sandwich Islands," said our geographer. He looked up at our flag, and noticed that it was floating toward the west, showing like a vane the direction of the wind.

" It is the trade wind," said he; " if we go toward the west it will carry us right along, but if we go toward the east it will hinder us."

We had a feeling as if we were going home when our faces were turned toward the Sandwich Islands, for there are so many Americans there, and we confidently expect that some day there will be a star on our flag for the state of the Sandwich Islands! Long before we reached there we saw smoke ascending from Mauna-Loa as from a furnace; and indeed, that is just what it is, being a volcano, where fires are nearly always aglow. We landed in the suburbs of Honolulu, the greatest city of the islands. Ready to greet us was a very distinguished looking personage. though he was hardly more than two feet high. His beautiful cape of tiny golden feathers showed us that he was a person of rank, and we were not at all surprised when he gave as his name " Prince Liholiho." We did not need to tell him what our errand was, for Erramongo had acquainted him with it, and he had heard also from Kassappu. He said:

A Sandwich Islands Brownie.

"You know of Captain Cook? He it was who brought the white man's drink to our islands; from that time until the missionaries came there was terrible drunkenness here; even the king was a drunkard. But the missionaries taught our people temperance, and laws were made that it should not be manufactured or sold. It was better here than elsewhere until one day a French ship came in, and the captain made our king sign an agreement to let French people bring their liquors to our islands to sell. Then there was drunkenness everywhere again."

"Is nothing being done for temperance now?"

"Yes," he said; "the missionaries and the native Christians are teaching temperance; and perhaps you have heard of Mrs. Mary Clement Leavitt; she has been here, and now the women of our country have a temperance society, and we believe this will yet be a temperate nation."

"We hope so," we said; "and we just wish we had the power to require all of your people to sign a temperance pledge before they become American citizens."

"Is that the way you do it in the United States?"

"Well, no, not exactly," we had to confess.

"Good-by, Prince Liholiho."

We had been so long in tropical regions it was proposed that we should now go where we could cool off. How would Iceland and Greenland do?

"Do? Just the thing," we all shouted in chorus.

A Greenland Brownie.

We suited the action to the word by pulling our furs out of the little cuddies which lined our flying ship all around the inside. We might easily have been taken for a company of Esquimaux, or perhaps for the exploring party who are on their way to the North Pole. As night came on a marvelous light filled the sky and "shined the little stars away." It flashed and flamed across the whole heavens. It was the Aurora Borealis.

Our good friend the geographer seemed to know just where we should land ; and so when we alighted on *terra firma* it was within sight of the settlement of Sukkertoppen. When our little brownie friend appeared, we saw that he was smaller than any we had yet seen—not half the length of my arm. He introduced himself to us as Eric Hernhut. His name showed that he was not an Esquimau, but a Dane.

"Greenland is such a cold country, we suppose there must be a great deal of liquor used," we said.

"You are mistaken," he said. "Greenlanders know that if they want to keep warm they must let liquor alone, and besides," said he, "they could not get it if they would, because Greenland is a prohibition country. There is only one day in the year when anybody can have any liquor to drink."

"When is that ? " we asked in surprise.

"On the king's birthday every man who wishes it may go to the government storehouse and get a glass of schnapps to drink the king's health."

We laughed ; we could not help it. Very bad health we should think the king might have with so many people taking poison in his name.

"Do the brownies drink schnapps on the king's birthday ? "

"Of course we do not. We drink to his health with good pure water; for we belong to the Brownies' World's Temperance Society."

"Do you ever visit the brownies in Iceland ? "

"Yes," he answered ; "Iceland is only 160 miles away, and that is no distance at all to a brownie."

"Neither is it a long distance for folks in a flying ma-

chine," we replied; and as soon as we had said our fare-
well we were off, and Eric Hernhut looked to us like only
a speck as we saw him speeding away on his reindeer.

Almost as quick as thought—well, as quick as two or
three thoughts—we had reached Iceland at Reikiavik, the
capital. We looked around expecting to find ice-palaces,
but not one met our eye; but in-
stead plenty of churches and com-
fortable houses.

"My name is Eyvind Thorgils-
son," said the quaint little brownie
who greeted us. "You will not find
a saloon in all Iceland," he said.

"Wonderful!" we all exclaimed.
"How can that be?" we asked.

"We have a Christian people
here," he answered.

He saw our look of surprise and
smiled as he said: "I think you
hardly expected to find civilized
people here." We had to confess
that it was so.

"Why," he continued, "Iceland

An Iceland Brownie.

had her millennial celebration about two years before you
had your centennial. Compare 1,000 years with 100!"

"Do you really mean to say that nobody in Iceland takes
strong drink?" we asked.

"No," he answered; "I cannot say that, because some
do have liquor in their homes; but it is a fact that there
are no saloons and no jails in Iceland."

"We are glad to learn you have such a happy people,
and we wish Americans had as good morals as Icelanders.
Good-by."

CHAPTER XI.

SWITZERLAND AND AUSTRIA.

WE were quite loth to leave Nature's refrigerator these hot summer days, and so it was proposed that we set wing for Switzerland. We decided that our landing-place should be the famous Chamouni Valley, above which rises the snow-covered peak of Mount Blanc, like a table set for the Sacrament.

We were so lost in looking upward that we hardly heard the tiny voice of our little brownie friend bidding us welcome to Switzerland. He looked like a mere speck in that great valley. "Emil Stauffacher greets you, and all the brownies welcome you." We looked about us, and hundreds, yes thousands, of elf-like faces were peering at us from behind the rocks, which were on every side. We noticed Emil's soldier-like garb, and said, "We hoped Swiss brownies did not fight." He drew himself proudly up and said: "Our people have always been brave—so brave that other nations have been glad to have them fight for them." "We have not come to talk about war, but temperance, dear friend," we said. "Do people in your country drink wine and beer, and do you have drunkards in Switzerland!" "Alas, yes," he answered; "there are nearly twenty-two thousand places in Switzerland where drink is sold, so you must know there are plenty of drunkards." "Is nothing being done for temperance in Switzerland?"

A Swiss Brownie.

"Oh, yes," answered Emil; "twenty years ago a teetotal temperance society was organized called 'Société de la Croix Bleu' (the Society of the Blue Cross)." We thought of the red cross on the Swiss flag, and asked whether or not the government was doing anything for temperance. "Oh, yes," replied Emil; "they think they are, by taking charge of the business themselves." "Ah, yes; then the liquor trade is conducted by the Société de la Croix Roth (red cross)?" "The brownies are the only folks in Switzerland who believe in prohibition," said Emil. "How wise you are!" we said, as we waved him good-by.

"Austria is the next door among nations; let us make a flying visit there," said the geographer of our party. It was thought a wise thing for us to do, because Austria is considered one of the greatest beer and wine-producing countries in the world. Indeed, we almost feared that the brownies themselves might take a drop now and then, as they would surely be told the lie that such light liquors are temperance drinks, and never make drunkards! We will go and see for ourselves. True as steel, a temperance brownie came forth to meet us. We looked for his temperance badge, and there it was pinned on his breast, with the letters we had learned to know so well—B. W. T. S. (Brownies' World Temperance Society). No beer and wine for him. He introduced himself as *Franz Windischgrätz*. What

An Austrian Brownie.

a name! "Does everybody in Austria drink beer and wine?" we asked. "I am proud to say," he answered, "that some of the officers in our army were the first to give up wine.   They used to have wine at their messes, but now they will not have it any more." Are there any other friends of temperance?" we asked.   "Yes," he answered; "some of the richest and highest class people are beginning to be more temperate." "Is there really much drunkenness in Austria?" we asked.   "Yes, yes," he answered; "in the very parts where the most beer and wine are made there are the most drunkards, and the fights and brawls are terrible."   "We need not ask you what you think of beer and wine as temperance drinks?"   "Brownies' heads are very small," said he, "but they contain enough sense to know that is a trade-lie."   As we glanced around, and in every direction, and saw the vine-clad hills, we were reminded of "the drunkards of Ephraim, whose glorious beauty is a fading flower, which are on the head of the fat valleys of them that are overcome with wine." "The crown of pride, the drunkards of Ephraim, shall be trodden under foot."   "You must do what you can for Austria, you temperance brownies," we said, as we said good-by to Franz Windischgrätz.

<h2 style="text-align:center">WINE   IS   A   MOCKER.</h2>

Yes, and beer is like unto it.

CHAPTER XII.

PALESTINE AND COREA.

THERE are two or three spots we must visit before we leave " the Old World," insisted one of our company. It seemed to the rest of us that we had been about everywhere, and we were beginning to have longing thoughts of home. "No, there is Palestine, 'the land of corn and wine,' and there is Corea, 'the hermit nation'; they have certainly never had any visitors drop down upon them from the sky. They can have no barriers skyward, so I think we shall be able to effect an entrance. We must visit both of these nations before we turn our faces to the coast," insisted our fellow-traveler. "Shall we skim the sea over, or shall we go overland?" asked our pilot. It was decided that we should fly over the Mediterranean Sea. The seascape below us looked for all the world like a blue sky underneath, instead of above, and the white sail-ships seemed to be great birds winging their way. Jerusalem was our destination, and we could but wonder what sort of brownies we should find there, as the people in Palestine are from almost every tribe and nation in

A Palestine Brownie.

the world. We did not know what to expect, but we were surprised to have a brownie greet us dressed as a shepherd. When we told him so, he replied by asking us if we had never read that shepherds were the oldest inhabitants, and we remembered that nobody can tell how old brownies are. "If you stay out on the hills watching the sheep, we fear you cannot tell us much about the temperance question," we said. "Oh, yes," he replied; "we keep watch of the vineyards, too, and once in a while we skip through those two big breweries over in Jaffa, just to see how much beer they are making." "Do they make all of the beer drank in Palestine?" "No," he answered, "it is brought in large quantities from Austria and Germany." "How about the wine; is that made in Palestine?" "About seventy bottles out of one hundred," he answered, "and *arak* is made, too, out of grapes and figs." "Surely Palestine cannot be called a land of temperance, as we have heard." "No, indeed," replied our shepherd brownie; "the Jews not only drink, but they are the liquor-sellers of the land. The Mohammedans, on the whole, are the most temperate people, and yet they do drink some wine and beer." "Is there no one doing anything for temperance in Palestine?" we asked. "Yes," he replied, "the missionaries are doing what they can; but what are they among so many drunkards, especially when our land is in the hands of the Turk? The Turkish Government collects taxes from anybody and everybody who sells liquor. Of course, the Turks are glad to see the trade increase." "May you live long enough to see Palestine a temperance land," we said in parting. "I hope so," he replied, "and I may have a different story to tell when you come again."

If we had to travel by steamer or by train, Corea would indeed be a long journey from Palestine; but by way of the sky, or "as the crow flies," we count it almost as nothing. We thought it best not to make our descent until night, for we knew that in the day-time our flying machine would attract the curious gaze, if not the warlike acts, of such a peculiar people as the Coreans. So along in the dead of night we settled down in the suburbs of Wiju. We had heard that nearly all of the families of that town made their living in liquor-selling, and we wanted to see with our eyes if it were so.   We found it so indeed.

"Here is one of the 'hermits,' surely," we whispered to each other as we caught sight of a most curious little brownie coming out to meet us.   Although it was night, he wore his large lace-like hat. His hat and fan and cane seemed to be as much a part of him as his very hands and eyes. He did not tip his hat—he simply could not—but he bowed politely and said: "*Kao-li Piengyang*." That we took to be his name, and bowed politely in return, saying: "We are an American temperance party." "Oh, yes," he replied; "I have been expecting to see you ever since I heard you were in Japan and China." "You do not care much to see strangers in Corea, do you?" we asked.   We were surprised when he replied, "We have seen a good many Ameri-

A Corean Brownie.

cans in Corea during the last fourteen years."   "Temperance parties?"   "No," he replied; "they brought their drink along with them, and it seemed to be stronger than anything we have in Corea."   "What do people in Corea make their liquor out of?"   "Rice and millet and barley." "Is there much drunkenness in Corea?" we asked.   "Yes, yes," he replied, sadly; "our people look old even while they are young, and it is considered honorable to get drunk.   Our great men may get drunk at dinner, and roll down by the table, and nobody says 'Shame,' but rather, 'How lucky he is to be rich enough to get drunk.'"   "Is no one doing anything for temperance in Corea?" we

asked. "The missionaries are doing what they can. They try to have our people grow tea to drink, instead of wine and other liquors." "And what does the government do?" "Nothing," said *Kao-li*, "excepting when the crop of grain is not large the people are not allowed to use much of it for liquor." "A small crop, then, must be a blessing to Corea," we ventured to say. "Yes, from the temperance point of view it is." Then he looked as though he was about to ask a question about the United States Government and temperance, and as there were some things we did not care about telling him, we made haste to be off.

CHAPTER XIII.

SOUTH AMERICA AND MEXICO.

SOUTH AMERICA was our next destination. We could reach it by going either to the east or west. How strange that two opposite directions would at last bring us to the same spot. That is because our world is round, you see. To go west we should have to fly over the hot country of India and over the Great Desert in Africa. Of course we could rise high enough to escape the heat, but we had always kept as near the earth as possible, so as not to have quite so far to fall, if fall we must. To go toward the east we should have entirely a sea trip, so we decided to go that way. We were interested to see Venezuela first, because of the much-talked-over boundary. We had not been able to send any word by the hermit brownie of Corea, and we found ourselves in quite a quandary about how we should reach the brownies. "Sing a temperance song," some one suggested.

A Venezuela Brownie.

Before our song was ended we saw little faces peering at us from behind the rocks and trees, and one little fellow became the spokesmen for the rest and came out to greet us—"Jose Martinez." "Do you have drunkards in Venezuela?" was our first question. "Why, yes; they have them everywhere, don't they?" he asked. And then he added : "We do not have such a lot of them as some other countries do, because it is so hot here people are afraid to drink much liquor." "How is it in other parts of South America where it is not so hot?" "Well, over in Brazil there are about fifty breweries, and they make wine there, too; lots of drunkards there." "What about the other parts of South America?" "Well, Argentine Republic is the worst of all The people there make wine, and beer, and rum; but they can't make all they want, they want so much, so they send to France for more. Would you believe it," he continued, "there are some men who pay a license fee of $1,250 a year, and yet they keep right on with their business of selling liquor." "Yes," we said; "we never did think high license would stop the liquor business, for it does not cost much to mix up drinks; a few cents' worth of stuff will make five gallons of brandy or five gallons of wine. You can't make the license high enough to make liquor men feel it." Jose said they had no temperance laws in South America. "Some day we hope there will be a federation of American republics, and that a prohibitory law will be one of the articles."

"Mexico is South America's nearest neighbor. The great gulf between them is the Gulf of Mexico, but it is easily covered with a flying machine. "Meet us in the Almeda in the quiet hour just after midnight" was the message we had sent the Mexican brownies by our friend Jose. You must know that the Almeda is the principal promenade in the city of Mexico, and at any other hour than in the dead of night brownies would hardly have dared to be seen there, and surely people in a flying machine would not want to land in broad daylight, with thousands of upturned faces watching them. When we had landed, on all sides we saw brownies peering at us through the branches of the great beech trees that line the sides of the Almeda, and some were sporting in the waters of the eleven foun-

tains. As brownie came forward to greet us he fairly
shone, so bright was the gold lace all down the sides of his
pantaloons.   We saw, too, that he had on great spurs that
rattled as he walked.   "My name is Miguel de Trejade,"
he said. " Mexico has not
been so honored before
as to receive a visit from
the friends of temper-
ance." " We are sorry
to have heard that there
is much drunkenness in
Mexico," we said; "is it
true?" "Yes, yes," he replied; "our people have
so much to make liquor
out of." " What do they
make it of?" " Have you
not heard about the
maguey plant?" he asked.
When we shook our
heads he said, " You call
it in your country 'the
century plant,' I have
heard." " Yes, but it is a

A Mexican Brownie.

very rare plant with us," we replied. "It grows everywhere in Mexico, and out of it our people make thread,
cloth, bagging, rope, paper, brooms, brushes, and combs."
" What a useful plant," we said. "Yes, yes," sadly answered Miguel; "but our people make it a fountain of sin
and sorrow, for when they see the blossom coming they
cut it out, making a kind of basin, and into this flows the
sap. As much as two quarts a day can be gathered from
each plant for two or three months. The sap thus gathered is fermented and made into a kind of liquor called
pulque.   It makes people very drunk.   In the city of Mexico alone as much as 300,000 pints of pulque are drank

every day.   On the railroads 'pulque trains' are run daily.
And that is not all," continued Miguel; "a very strong
kind of liquor is made from the leaves of the maguey."
" Are there no laws against the making of these drinks ? "
we asked.   "No," he answered; "each person who sells
pulque must have a license, that is all."   " Is no one doing
anything for temperance in Mexico?" we asked.   "Yes,
the missionaries preach temperance and sometimes our
newspapers have something to say about it."   " What do
the brownies do about the maguey ? "   " They use it only
for good purposes," he replied.   We were glad that the
maguey is only a rare plant in the United States.

CHAPTER XIV.

CANADA AND RETURN TO THE UNITED STATES, LANDING IN NEW YORK CITY.

MEXICO is our next-door neighbor on the south and Canada is our next-door neighbor on the north. Having paid our respects to our neighbor on the south, before we go home we must make a call on our northern neighbor, and inquire into the state of her body, temperance.

We had heard what a noble class of people live in Toronto, so we thought we would make that our stopping-place. As it was in the winter, we were not at all surprised to have our brownie friend come forth to meet us clad in his toboggan suit and snowshoes. He directed us to follow him, and he would guide us where we could see the whole brownie tribe. They seemed to be spilling promiscuously down the great slide, and their merry laugh sounded like the jingling of sleighbells. They invited us to a slide, but we declined. "Robert MacArthur is my name," said our brownie guide, "and I will be pleased to answer any questions about temperance in Canada." "Tell us what 'plebiscites' are," we said. "We have heard that you have them up here in Canada." "I suppose you are thinking of

A Canadian Brownie.

the temperance plebiscites," he replied. " It means that people are given a chance to vote whether or not they want the government to close the saloons in Canada and have prohibition. All but one of the provinces in Canada have voted, and they all want prohibition," he replied, and swung his toque. " Is Toronto a temperance city?" we asked. " You will think so when I tell you that our Mayor and seven Aldermen are prohibitionists," he answered. " That is not quite what we are used to in the United States," we said in an undertone, as we glanced at each other. " You could hardly say such good things of the

Washington Arch.

people as far west as Manitoba, could you?" There was a twinkle in his eye as he answered : " Nearly all the members of their Legislature are prohibitionists." " Whew !" we exclaimed; "we never saw it in this wise. How glad we are to have such good neighbors ! Good-day !"

At last our faces were turned homeward, and we concluded to make a landing in New York just beside the

Washington Arch. It was a favorite spot with us, because of the grand motto engraved upon it, the words of our greatest hero, George Washington :

> **Let us raise a standard to which the wise and the honest may repair. The event is in the hand of God.**

How could a nation live up to that motto without temperance law?

Our Uncle Sam himself was at the arch to meet us. "Glad to welcome you home, my children," said he. "You found the eagle's wings strong and true, didn't you?"

"Have you some good temperance news for us, Uncle Sam?" "Yes, first rate," he said, as he wiped his forehead with his bandana pocket-handkerchief. "My boys and girls are all taught temperance in the day-school." "All, all, Uncle Sam?" "All except in Virginia and Georgia and Arkansas. I said 'all' because I expect they'll soon be in the ring." "How did that come about?" we asked. "Why, the Legislatures were worked for it," he said. "And in the Sunday-schools four temperance lessons a year are taught there." "Why, Uncle Sam, we are just grow-

Uncle Sam.

ing temperance statesmen, aren't we?" "Yes, indeedy; we are sure to have prohibition when my boys and girls grow up." "How many prohibition States have we now,

Uncle Sam?" "Six in the North, and lots of prohibition counties in the South. The temperance sentiment is growing in every direction; churches won't take rumsellers in for members; railroads won't employ men who drink; great dinners are now given without a drop of wine by people connected with the government; our people are proud to wear temperance bows and temperance buttons; some of the finest orators in our land speak for temperance." We were rejoiced to hear these signs of the times, and we said, "Uncle Sam, we have the best country on earth, and we have come back to try to make it still better by working to pledge its twenty millions of children to total abstinence and prohibition.

> " Tremble, King Alcohol,
> They will grow up."

Cheap Temperance Literature.

LOW PRICES TO SUIT THE TIMES.

The National Temperance Society have recently issued a number of their standard works in paper covers, for general circulation among the masses, at prices within the reach of all.

Alcohol and the State. 12mo, 411 pp. By R. C. Pitman, LL.D. What Alcohol does to the State, and what the State ought to do to Alcohol..................................... ....$0 50

Bread and Beer. 12mo, 381 pages. By Mary Dwinell Chellis. A thrilling story full of argument and illustration............ 50

Prohibitionist's Text-Book, The. 12mo, 312 pp......... .. 50

Our Wasted Resources; or, The Missing Link in the Temperance Reform. By William Hargreaves, M.D. 12mo, 202 pp... 50

Ten Lectures on Alcohol. By B. W. Richardson, M.D 12mo, 338 pp. Comprising "Cantor Lectures," "Alcohol on the Body and the Mind," "Moderate Drinking," and "The Liberty of the Abject.". 50

Talks on Temperance. 12mo, 198 pp. By Canon Farrar, D.D. This book contains ten sermons and talks by this eminent divine. 25

Liquor Laws of the United States, revised and corrected, together with Extracts from Decisions of the Courts in New York, New Jersey, etc. 12mo, 138 pp 25

Moderation vs. Total Abstinence; or, Dr. Crosby and his Reviewers. 12mo, 126 pp. Containing addresses by Howard Crosby, D.D., Mark Hopkins, D.D., Wendell Phillips, T. L. Cuyler, D.D., Mrs. J. E. Foster, etc 25

Readings and Recitations, No. 1. 12mo, 96 pp. By Miss L. Penney. A choice collection of Prose and Verse, suitable for Declamations, Public or Parlor Readings, etc........................ 25

Readings and Recitations, No. 2. 12mo, 96 pp. By Miss L. Penney.......... 25

Readings and Recitations, No. 3. 12mo, 96 pp. By Miss L. Penney....... 25

Alcohol and Hygiene. An Elementary Lesson-Book for Schools. 12mo, 234 pp. By Julia Colman. author of "The Catechism on Alcohol," "Juvenile Temperance Manual," etc.................... 30

Bible Wines; or, The Laws of Fermentation and Wines of the Ancients. 12mo, 139 pp. By Wm Patton, D.D.............. 25

Evangelistic Temperance Work. 12mo, 34 pp. By Mrs. S. M. I. Henry....................... 15

Prohibition Does Prohibit; or, Prohibition not a Failure. 12mo, 48 pp. By J. N. Stearns.... 10

The Trial of John Barleycorn by a Jury of Twelve Men Fifteen Witnesses. 26 pp......... 10

A
TOUR AROUND THE WORLD

AMONG THE

TEMPERANCE BROWNIES.

WITH BLACKBOARD ILLUSTRATIONS.

BY

MRS. WILBUR F. CRAFTS,

AUTHOR OF "BLACKBOARD TEMPERANCE LESSONS," NOS. 1, 2, 3, ETC.

NEW YORK:

The National Temperance Society and Publication House,

58 READE STREET.

NEW TEMPERANCE PUBLICATIONS.

THE NATIONAL TEMPERANCE SOCIETY publishes over 2,000 different publica tions upon every phase of the temperance question, adapted to every line of work, every department of life, and for all kinds of temperance organizations. The following are specially adapted to public Readings, Recitations, Dialogues, Cantatas, Songs, etc., for Temperance Meetings, Lodge and Division Meetings, etc.

The Temperance Platform. Prepared by Miss L. Penney. Large 12mo, 120 pages. Cloth, **50** cents ; paper.. . ... **.25**

This contains Orations on Total Abstinence and Prohibition, especially adapted to Prize Contests, Public Meetings, and Social Gatherings, by noted advocates of the cause. The best collection ever made.

Readings and Recitations Combined. By Miss L. Penney. 12mo. 528 pages. Bound in cloth, only.............. .... **1.00**

Being Readings and Recitations Nos. 1, 2, 3, 4, and 5 bound together in one volume.

A Temperance Picnic with the Old Woman who Lived in A SHOE. By Mrs. Nellie H. Bradley........................... .... **.25**

One of the most unique and pleasing entertainments ever published for the children, in the style of a cantata; containing bright, taking music for solos and choruses ; Recitations, Colloquies, etc.

An Hour with Mother Goose and Her Temperance Family. By Mrs. Nellie H. Bradley.................................... .... **.25**

An entertaining and instructive entertainment for young people, giving Solos, Duets, Choruses, Recitations, Colloquies, etc., for well-known Mother Goose characters.

Concert Temperance Exercises; OR, HELPS FOR ENTERTAINMENTS. By Miss L. Penney. 16mo, 160 pages. Paper, **25** cents ; cloth........ **.50**

The Temperance Speaker. By J. N. Stearns. 288 pages. Paper, **.25** Cloth... .... **.50**

Blackboard Temperance Lessons, No. 5. By Mrs. W. F. Crafts. 16mo .... **.10**

A new collection of chalk-talks with skilful blackboard designs. Designed for use in Sunday-schools and all children's organizations.

Rallying Songs for Young Teetotalers. 80 pages. Price, per dozen, **$1.50;** single copy...................... .... **.15**

Enlarged edition, 14 new pages added, making it the best and most complete children's song-book of the day.

An Evening with Robinson Crusoe. By Julia Colman. Per dozen, 60 cents ; single copy.. .. .. **.05**

A novel entertainment. in which a number of young people can take part. Several choice songs add to its attraction.

Catechism on Alcohol and Tobacco. 16mo, 32 pages, 5 cents ; per dozen..... .... **.60**

Juvenile Temperance Reciter, No. 3. By Miss L. Penney. 16mo, 64 pages.... ....·..... **.10**

A new series of Concert Exercises has been commenced containing individual and class Recitations, Responsive Exercises, singing, with choice pieces of music, with notes and words. 8vo, 16 pages. Only 5 cents each ; **$4.00** per 100.

No. 1.—What shall the Harvest be ? By Mrs. G. A. Hewitt.
No. 2.—Alcohol our Enemy. By J. N. Stearns.
No. 3.—King Alcohol. A Burlesque. By A. J. Foxwell.
No. 4.—The Two Invitations. By Thos. R. Thompson.
No. 5.—Our Standards. By Thos. R. Thompson.

NEW TEMPERANCE PUBLICATIONS.